FOREWORD

The collection of "Everything Will Be Okay" travel phrasebooks published by T&P Books is designed for people traveling abroad for tourism and business. The phrasebooks contain what matters most - the essentials for basic communication. This is an indispensable set of phrases to "survive" while abroad.

This phrasebook will help you in most cases where you need to ask something, get directions, find out how much something costs, etc. It can also resolve difficult communication situations where gestures just won't help.

This book contains a lot of phrases that have been grouped according to the most relevant topics. You'll also find a mini dictionary with useful words - numbers, time, calendar, colors...

Take "Everything Will Be Okay" phrasebook with you on the road and you'll have an irreplaceable traveling companion who will help you find your way out of any situation and teach you to not fear speaking with foreigners.

TABLE OF CONTENTS

T&P Books Publishing

Travel phrasebooks collection
«Everything Will Be Okay!»

T&P Books Publishing

PHRASEBOOK

— FRENCH —

By Andrey Taranov

THE MOST IMPORTANT PHRASES

This phrasebook contains
the most important
phrases and questions
for basic communication
Everything you need
to survive overseas

T&P BOOKS

Phrasebook + 250-word dictionary

English-French phrasebook & mini dictionary

By Andrey Taranov

The collection of "Everything Will Be Okay" travel phrasebooks published by T&P Books is designed for people traveling abroad for tourism and business. The phrasebooks contain what matters most - the essentials for basic communication. This is an indispensable set of phrases to "survive" while abroad.

You'll also find a mini dictionary with 250 useful words required for everyday communication - the names of months and days of the week, measurements, family members, and more.

T&P Books Publishing
www.tpbooks.com

ISBN: 978-1-78492-420-1

This book is also available in E-book formats.
Please visit www.tpbooks.com or the major online bookstores.

PRONUNCIATION

Letter	French example	T&P phonetic alphabet	English example

Vowels

Letter	French example	T&P phonetic alphabet	English example
A a	cravate	[a]	shorter than in ask
E e	mer	[ɛ]	man, bad
I i [1]	hier	[j]	yes, New York
I i [2]	musique	[i]	shorter than in feet
O o	porte	[o], [ɔ]	drop, baught
U u	rue	[y]	fuel, tuna
Y y [3]	yacht	[j]	yes, New York
Y y [4]	type	[i]	shorter than in feet

Consonants

Letter	French example	T&P phonetic alphabet	English example
B b	robe	[b]	baby, book
C c [5]	place	[s]	city, boss
C c [6]	canard	[k]	clock, kiss
Ç ç	leçon	[s]	city, boss
D d	disque	[d]	day, doctor
F f	femme	[f]	face, food
G g [7]	page	[ʒ]	forge, pleasure
G g [8]	gare	[g]	game, gold
H h	héros	[h]	silent [h]
J j	jour	[ʒ]	forge, pleasure
K k	kilo	[k]	clock, kiss
L l	aller	[l]	lace, people
M m	maison	[m]	magic, milk
N n	nom	[n]	name, normal
P p	papier	[p]	pencil, private
Q q	cinq	[k]	clock, kiss
R r	mars	[r]	rolled [r]
S s [9]	raison	[z]	zebra, please
S s [10]	sac	[s]	city, boss
T t	table	[t]	tourist, trip
V v	verre	[v]	very, river
W w	Taïwan	[w]	vase, winter

Letter	French example	T&P phonetic alphabet	English example
X x [11]	expliquer	[ks]	box, taxi
X x [12]	exact	[gz]	exam, exact
X x [13]	dix	[s]	city, boss
X x [14]	dixième	[z]	zebra, please
Z z	zéro	[z]	zebra, please

Combinations of letters

ai	faire	[ɛ]	man, bad
au	faute	[o], [oː]	floor, doctor
ay	payer	[eɪ]	age, today
ei	treize	[ɛ]	man, bad
eau	eau	[o], [oː]	floor, doctor
eu	beurre	[ø]	eternal, church
œ	œil	[ø]	eternal, church
œu	cœur	[øː]	first, thirsty
ou	nous	[u]	book
oi	noir	[wa]	watt, white
oy	voyage	[wa]	watt, white
qu	quartier	[k]	clock, kiss
ch	chat	[ʃ]	machine, shark
th	thé	[t]	tourist, trip
ph	photo	[f]	face, food
gu [15]	guerre	[g]	game, gold
ge [16]	géographie	[ʒ]	forge, pleasure
gn	ligne	[ɲ]	canyon, new
on, om	maison, nom	[ɔ̃]	strong

Comments

[1] before vowels
[2] elsewhere
[3] before vowels
[4] elsewhere
[5] before e, i, y
[6] elsewhere
[7] before e, i, y
[8] elsewhere
[9] between two vowels

[10] elsewhere
[11] most of cases
[12] rarely
[13] in dix, six, soixante
[14] in dixième, sixième
[15] before e, i, u
[16] before a, o, y

LIST OF ABBREVIATIONS

English abbreviations

ab.	-	about
adj	-	adjective
adv	-	adverb
anim.	-	animate
as adj	-	attributive noun used as adjective
e.g.	-	for example
etc.	-	et cetera
fam.	-	familiar
fem.	-	feminine
form.	-	formal
inanim.	-	inanimate
masc.	-	masculine
math	-	mathematics
mil.	-	military
n	-	noun
pl	-	plural
pron.	-	pronoun
sb	-	somebody
sing.	-	singular
sth	-	something
v aux	-	auxiliary verb
vi	-	intransitive verb
vi, vt	-	intransitive, transitive verb
vt	-	transitive verb

French abbreviations

adj	-	adjective
adv	-	adverb
conj	-	conjunction
etc.	-	et cetera
f	-	feminine noun
f pl	-	feminine plural
m	-	masculine noun
m pl	-	masculine plural
m, f	-	masculine, feminine

pl	-	plural
prep	-	preposition
pron	-	pronoun
v aux	-	auxiliary verb
v imp	-	impersonnel verb
vi	-	intransitive verb
vi, vt	-	intransitive, transitive verb
vp	-	pronominal verb
vt	-	transitive verb

T&P BOOKS

FRENCH PHRASEBOOK

This section contains
important phrases that may
come in handy in various
real-life situations.
The phrasebook will help
you ask for directions, clarify
a price, buy tickets, and
order food at a restaurant

T&P Books Publishing

PHRASEBOOK
CONTENTS

T&P Books Publishing

The bare minimum

Excuse me, ...	**Excusez-moi, ...** [ɛkskyze mwa, ...]
Hello.	**Bonjour** [bõʒuːr]
Thank you.	**Merci** [mɛrsi]
Good bye.	**Au revoir** [o rəvwaːr]
Yes.	**Oui** [wi]
No.	**Non** [nõ]
I don't know.	**Je ne sais pas.** [ʒə nə sɛ pɑ]
Where? | Where to? | When?	**Où? | Où? | Quand?** [u? | u? | kɑ̃?]
I need ...	**J'ai besoin de ...** [ʒe bəzwɛ̃ də ...]
I want ...	**Je veux ...** [ʒə vø ...]
Do you have ...?	**Avez-vous ... ?** [ave vu ...?]
Is there a ... here?	**Est-ce qu'il y a ... ici?** [ɛs kilja ... isi?]
May I ...?	**Puis-je ... ?** [pɥiʒ ...?]
..., please (polite request)	**..., s'il vous plaît** [..., sil vu plɛ]
I'm looking for ...	**Je cherche ...** [ʒə ʃɛrʃ ...]
restroom	**les toilettes** [le twalɛt]
ATM	**un distributeur** [œ̃ distribytœːr]
pharmacy (drugstore)	**une pharmacie** [yn farmasi]
hospital	**l'hôpital** [lɔpital]
police station	**le commissariat de police** [lə kɔmisarja də polis]
subway	**une station de métro** [yn stasjõ də metro]

taxi	**un taxi** [œ̃ taksi]
train station	**la gare** [la gar]

My name is ...	**Je m'appelle ...** [ʒə mapɛl ...]
What's your name?	**Comment vous appelez-vous?** [kɔmɑ̃ vuzaple-vu?]
Could you please help me?	**Aidez-moi, s'il vous plaît.** [ɛde-mwa, sil vu plɛ]
I've got a problem.	**J'ai un problème.** [ʒe œ̃ prɔblɛm]
I don't feel well.	**Je ne me sens pas bien.** [ʒə nə mə sɑ̃ pɑ bjɛ̃]
Call an ambulance!	**Appelez une ambulance!** [aple yn ɑ̃bylɑ̃:s!]
May I make a call?	**Puis-je faire un appel?** [pɥiʒ fɛr œn apɛl?]

I'm sorry.	**Excusez-moi.** [ɛkskyze mwa]
You're welcome.	**Je vous en prie.** [ʒə vuzɑ̃pri]

I, me	**je, moi** [ʒə, mwa]
you (inform.)	**tu, toi** [ty, twa]
he	**il** [il]
she	**elle** [ɛl]
they (masc.)	**ils** [il]
they (fem.)	**elles** [ɛl]
we	**nous** [nu]
you (pl)	**vous** [vu]
you (sg, form.)	**Vous** [vu]

ENTRANCE	**ENTRÉE** [ɑ̃tre]
EXIT	**SORTIE** [sɔrti]
OUT OF ORDER	**HORS SERVICE | EN PANNE** [ɔr sɛrvis | ɑ̃ pan]
CLOSED	**FERMÉ** [fɛrme]

OPEN	**OUVERT** [uvɛr]
FOR WOMEN	**POUR LES FEMMES** [pur le fam]
FOR MEN	**POUR LES HOMMES** [pur le zɔm]

Questions

Where?	**Où?** [u?]
Where to?	**Où?** [u?]
Where from?	**D'où?** [du?]
Why?	**Pourquoi?** [purkwa?]
For what reason?	**Pour quelle raison?** [pur kɛl rɛzõ?]
When?	**Quand?** [kɑ̃?]
How long?	**Combien de temps?** [kõbjɛ̃ də tɑ̃?]
At what time?	**À quelle heure?** [a kɛl œ:r?]
How much?	**C'est combien?** [sɛ kõbjɛ̃?]
Do you have ...?	**Avez-vous ... ?** [ave vu ...?]
Where is ...?	**Où est ..., s'il vous plaît?** [u ɛ ..., sil vu plɛ?]
What time is it?	**Quelle heure est-il?** [kɛl œr ɛ-til?]
May I make a call?	**Puis-je faire un appel?** [pɥiʒ fɛr œn apɛl?]
Who's there?	**Qui est là?** [ki ɛ la?]
Can I smoke here?	**Puis-je fumer ici?** [pɥiʒ fyme isi?]
May I ...?	**Puis-je ...?** [pɥiʒ ...?]

Needs

I'd like ...	**Je voudrais ...** [ʒə vudrɛ ...]
I don't want ...	**Je ne veux pas ...** [ʒə nə vø pa ...]
I'm thirsty.	**J'ai soif.** [ʒe swaf]
I want to sleep.	**Je veux dormir.** [ʒə vø dɔrmiːr]
I want ...	**Je veux ...** [ʒə vø ...]
to wash up	**me laver** [mə lave]
to brush my teeth	**brosser mes dents** [brɔse me dɑ̃]
to rest a while	**me reposer un instant** [mə rəpoze œn ɛ̃stɑ̃]
to change my clothes	**changer de vêtements** [ʃɑ̃ʒe də vɛtmɑ̃]
to go back to the hotel	**retourner à l'hôtel** [rəturne a lotɛl]
to buy ...	**acheter ...** [aʃte ...]
to go to ...	**aller à ...** [ale a ...]
to visit ...	**visiter ...** [vizite ...]
to meet with ...	**rencontrer ...** [rɑ̃kɔ̃tre ...]
to make a call	**faire un appel** [fɛr œn apɛl]
I'm tired.	**Je suis fatigué /fatiguée/** [ʒə sɥi fatige]
We are tired.	**Nous sommes fatigués /fatiguées/** [nu sɔm fatige]
I'm cold.	**J'ai froid.** [ʒe frwa]
I'm hot.	**J'ai chaud.** [ʒe ʃo]
I'm OK.	**Je suis bien.** [ʒə sɥi bjɛ̃]

I need to make a call.

Il me faut faire un appel.
[il mə fo fɛr œn apɛl]

I need to go to the restroom.

J'ai besoin d'aller aux toilettes.
[ʒe bəzwɛ̃ dale o twalɛt]

I have to go.

Il faut que j'aille.
[il fo kə ʒaj]

I have to go now.

Je dois partir maintenant.
[ʒə dwa partir mɛ̃tnɑ̃]

Asking for directions

Excuse me, ...	**Excusez-moi, ...** [ɛkskyze mwa, ...]
Where is ...?	**Où est ..., s'il vous plaît?** [u ɛ ..., sil vu plɛ?]
Which way is ...?	**Dans quelle direction est ... ?** [dɑ̃ kɛl dirɛksjɔ̃ ɛ ... ?]
Could you help me, please?	**Pouvez-vous m'aider, s'il vous plaît?** [puve vu mɛde, sil vu plɛ?]
I'm looking for ...	**Je cherche ...** [ʒə ʃɛrʃ ...]
I'm looking for the exit.	**La sortie, s'il vous plaît?** [la sɔrti, sil vu plɛ?]
I'm going to ...	**Je vais à ...** [ʒə ve a ...]
Am I going the right way to ...?	**C'est la bonne direction pour ...?** [sɛ la bɔn dirɛksjɔ̃ pur ...?]
Is it far?	**C'est loin?** [sɛ lwɛ̃?]
Can I get there on foot?	**Est-ce que je peux y aller à pied?** [ɛskə ʒə pø i ale a pje?]
Can you show me on the map?	**Pouvez-vous me le montrer sur la carte?** [puve vu mə lə mɔ̃tre syr la kart?]
Show me where we are right now.	**Montrez-moi où sommes-nous, s'il vous plaît.** [mɔ̃tre-mwa u sɔm-nu, sil vu plɛ]
Here	**Ici** [isi]
There	**Là-bas** [labɑ]
This way	**Par ici** [par isi]
Turn right.	**Tournez à droite.** [turne a drwat]
Turn left.	**Tournez à gauche.** [turne a goʃ]

first (second, third) turn

**Prenez la première
(deuxième, troisième) rue.**
[prəne la prəmjɛr
(døzjɛm, trwazjɛm) ry]

to the right

à droite
[a drwat]

to the left

à gauche
[a goʃ]

Go straight.

Continuez tout droit.
[kõtinɥe tu drwa]

Signs

WELCOME!	**BIENVENUE!** [bjɛ̃vny!]
ENTRANCE	**ENTRÉE** [ãtre]
EXIT	**SORTIE** [sɔrti]
PUSH	**POUSSEZ** [puse]
PULL	**TIREZ** [tire]
OPEN	**OUVERT** [uvɛr]
CLOSED	**FERMÉ** [fɛrme]
FOR WOMEN	**POUR LES FEMMES** [pur le fam]
FOR MEN	**POUR LES HOMMES** [pur le zɔm]
MEN, GENTS	**MESSIEURS (M)** [məsjø]
WOMEN, LADIES	**FEMMES (F)** [fam]
DISCOUNTS	**RABAIS	SOLDES** [rabɛ	sɔld]
SALE	**PROMOTION** [prɔmɔsjɔ̃]
FREE	**GRATUIT** [gratɥi]
NEW!	**NOUVEAU!** [nuvo!]
ATTENTION!	**ATTENTION!** [atɑ̃sjɔ̃!]
NO VACANCIES	**COMPLET** [kɔ̃plɛ]
RESERVED	**RÉSERVÉ** [rezɛrve]
ADMINISTRATION	**ADMINISTRATION** [administrasjɔ̃]
STAFF ONLY	**PERSONNEL SEULEMENT** [pɛrsɔnɛl sœlmɑ̃]

BEWARE OF THE DOG! | **ATTENTION AU CHIEN!**
[atɑ̃sjɔ̃ o ʃjɛ̃!]

NO SMOKING! | **NE PAS FUMER!**
[nə pɑ fyme!]

DO NOT TOUCH! | **NE PAS TOUCHER!**
[nə pɑ tuʃe!]

DANGEROUS | **DANGEREUX**
[dɑ̃ʒrø]

DANGER | **DANGER**
[dɑ̃ʒe]

HIGH VOLTAGE | **HAUTE TENSION**
[ot tɑ̃sjɔ̃]

NO SWIMMING! | **BAIGNADE INTERDITE!**
[bɛɲad ɛ̃tɛrdit!]

OUT OF ORDER | **HORS SERVICE | EN PANNE**
[ɔr sɛrvis | ɑ̃ pan]

FLAMMABLE | **INFLAMMABLE**
[ɛ̃flamabl]

FORBIDDEN | **INTERDIT**
[ɛ̃tɛrdi]

NO TRESPASSING! | **ENTRÉE INTERDITE!**
[ɑ̃tre ɛ̃tɛrdit!]

WET PAINT | **PEINTURE FRAÎCHE**
[pɛ̃tyr frɛʃ]

CLOSED FOR RENOVATIONS | **FERMÉ POUR TRAVAUX**
[fɛrme pur travɔ]

WORKS AHEAD | **TRAVAUX EN COURS**
[travɔ ɑ̃ kur]

DETOUR | **DÉVIATION**
[devjasjɔ̃]

Transportation. General phrases

plane	**avion** [avjɔ̃]
train	**train** [trɛ̃]
bus	**bus, autobus** [bys, otɔbys]
ferry	**ferry** [feri]
taxi	**taxi** [taksi]
car	**voiture** [vwatyr]
schedule	**horaire** [ɔrɛr]
Where can I see the schedule?	**Où puis-je voir l'horaire?** [u pɥiʒ vwar lɔrɛːr?]
workdays (weekdays)	**jours ouvrables** [ʒur uvrabl]
weekends	**jours non ouvrables** [ʒur nɔn uvrabl]
holidays	**jours fériés** [ʒur ferje]
DEPARTURE	**DÉPART** [depar]
ARRIVAL	**ARRIVÉE** [arive]
DELAYED	**RETARDÉE** [rətarde]
CANCELED	**ANNULÉE** [anyle]
next (train, etc.)	**prochain** [prɔʃɛ̃]
first	**premier** [prəmje]
last	**dernier** [dɛrnje]
When is the next ...?	**À quelle heure est le prochain ...?** [a kɛl œr ɛ lə prɔʃɛ̃ ...?]
When is the first ...?	**À quelle heure est le premier ...?** [a kɛl œr ɛ lə prəmje ...?]

When is the last ...?

À quelle heure est le dernier ...?
[a kɛl œr ɛ lə dɛrnje ...?]

transfer (change of trains, etc.)

correspondance
[kɔrɛspɔ̃dɑ̃s]

to make a transfer

prendre la correspondance
[prɑ̃dr la kɔrɛspɔ̃dɑ̃s]

Do I need to make a transfer?

Dois-je prendre la correspondance?
[dwaʒ prɑ̃dr la kɔrɛspɔ̃dɑ̃s?]

Buying tickets

Where can I buy tickets?	**Où puis-je acheter des billets?** [u pɥiʒ aʃte de bijɛ?]
ticket	**billet** [bijɛ]
to buy a ticket	**acheter un billet** [aʃte œ̃ bijɛ]
ticket price	**le prix d'un billet** [lə pri dœ̃ bijɛ]

Where to?	**Pour aller où?** [pur ale u?]
To what station?	**Quelle destination?** [kɛl dɛstinasjɔ̃?]
I need …	**Je voudrais …** [ʒə vudrɛ …]
one ticket	**un billet** [œ̃ bijɛ]
two tickets	**deux billets** [dø bijɛ]
three tickets	**trois billets** [trwɑ bijɛ]

one-way	**aller simple** [ale sɛ̃pl]
round-trip	**aller-retour** [ale-rətur]
first class	**première classe** [prəmjɛr klɑs]
second class	**classe économique** [klɑs ekɔnɔmik]

today	**aujourd'hui** [oʒurdɥi]
tomorrow	**demain** [dəmɛ̃]
the day after tomorrow	**après-demain** [aprɛdmɛ̃]
in the morning	**dans la matinée** [dɑ̃ la matine]
in the afternoon	**l'après-midi** [laprɛmidi]
in the evening	**dans la soirée** [dɑ̃ la sware]

aisle seat

siège côté couloir
[sjɛʒ kote kulwar]

window seat

siège côté fenêtre
[sjɛʒ kote fənɛtr]

How much?

C'est combien?
[sɛ kõbjɛ̃?]

Can I pay by credit card?

Puis-je payer avec la carte?
[pɥiʒ peje avɛk la kart?]

Bus

bus	**bus, autobus** [otɔbys]
intercity bus	**autocar** [otɔkar]
bus stop	**arrêt d'autobus** [arɛ dotɔbys]
Where's the nearest bus stop?	**Où est l'arrêt d'autobus** **le plus proche?** [u ɛ larɛ dotɔbys lə ply prɔʃ?]
number (bus ~, etc.)	**numéro** [nymero]
Which bus do I take to get to ...?	**Quel bus dois-je prendre** **pour aller à ...?** [kɛl bys dwaʒ prɑ̃dr pur ale a ...?]
Does this bus go to ...?	**Est-ce que ce bus va à ...?** [ɛskə sə bys va a ...?]
How frequent are the buses?	**L'autobus passe tous les combien?** [lotɔbys pɑs tu le kɔ̃bjɛ̃?]
every 15 minutes	**chaque quart d'heure** [ʃak kar dœr]
every half hour	**chaque demi-heure** [ʃak dəmiœr]
every hour	**chaque heure** [ʃak œr]
several times a day	**plusieurs fois par jour** [plyzjœr fwa par ʒur]
... times a day	**... fois par jour** [... fwa par ʒur]
schedule	**horaire** [ɔrɛr]
Where can I see the schedule?	**Où puis-je voir l'horaire?** [u pɥiʒ vwar lɔrɛːr?]
When is the next bus?	**À quelle heure passe le prochain bus?** [a kɛl œr pɑs lə prɔʃɛ̃ bys?]
When is the first bus?	**À quelle heure passe le premier bus?** [a kɛl œr pɑs lə prəmje bys?]
When is the last bus?	**À quelle heure passe le dernier bus?** [a kɛl œr pɑs lə dɛrnje bys?]

stop

arrêt
[arɛ]

next stop

prochain arrêt
[prɔʃɛn arɛ]

last stop (terminus)

terminus
[tɛrminys]

Stop here, please.

Pouvez-vous arrêter ici, s'il vous plaît.
[puve vu arɛte isi, sil vu plɛ]

Excuse me, this is my stop.

Excusez-moi, c'est mon arrêt.
[ɛkskyze mwa, sɛ mɔ̃n arɛ]

Train

train	**train** [trɛ̃]
suburban train	**train de banlieue** [trɛ̃ də bɑ̃ljø]
long-distance train	**train de grande ligne** [trɛ̃ də grɑ̃d liɲ]
train station	**la gare** [la gar]
Excuse me, where is the exit to the platform?	**Excusez-moi, où est la sortie vers les quais?** [ɛkskyze mwa, u ɛ la sɔrti vɛr le ke?]
Does this train go to …?	**Est-ce que ce train va à …?** [ɛskə sə trɛ̃ va a …?]
next train	**le prochain train** [lə prɔʃɛ̃ trɛ̃]
When is the next train?	**À quelle heure est le prochain train?** [a kɛl œr ɛ lə prɔʃɛ̃ trɛ̃?]
Where can I see the schedule?	**Où puis-je voir l'horaire?** [u pɥiʒ vwar lɔrɛ:r?]
From which platform?	**De quel quai?** [də kɛl ke?]
When does the train arrive in …?	**À quelle heure arrive le train à …?** [a kɛl œr ariv lə trɛ̃ a …?]
Please help me.	**Pouvez-vous m'aider, s'il vous plaît?** [puve-vu mɛde, sil vu plɛ?]
I'm looking for my seat.	**Je cherche ma place.** [ʒə ʃɛrʃ ma plas]
We're looking for our seats.	**Nous cherchons nos places.** [nu ʃɛrʃɔ̃ no plas]
My seat is taken.	**Ma place est occupée.** [ma plas ɛtokype]
Our seats are taken.	**Nos places sont occupées.** [no plas sɔ̃ ɔkype]
I'm sorry but this is my seat.	**Excusez-moi, mais c'est ma place.** [ɛkskyze mwa, mɛ sɛ ma plas]
Is this seat taken?	**Est-ce que cette place est libre?** [ɛskə sɛt plas ɛ li:br?]
May I sit here?	**Puis-je m'asseoir ici?** [pɥiʒ maswar isi?]

On the train. Dialogue (No ticket)

Ticket, please.
Votre billet, s'il vous plaît.
[vɔtr bijɛ, sil vu plɛ]

I don't have a ticket.
Je n'ai pas de billet.
[ʒə ne pɑ də bijɛ]

I lost my ticket.
J'ai perdu mon billet.
[ʒe pɛrdy mɔ̃ bijɛ]

I forgot my ticket at home.
J'ai oublié mon billet à la maison.
[ʒe ublije mɔ̃ bijɛ a la mɛzɔ̃]

You can buy a ticket from me.
Vous pouvez m'acheter un billet.
[vu puve maʃte œ̃ bijɛ]

You will also have to pay a fine.
Vous devrez aussi payer une amende.
[vu dəvre osi peje yn amɑ̃d]

Okay.
D'accord.
[dakɔ:r]

Where are you going?
Où allez-vous?
[u ale-vu?]

I'm going to …
Je vais à …
[ʒə ve a …]

How much? I don't understand.
Combien? Je ne comprend pas.
[kɔ̃bjɛ̃? ʒə nə kɔ̃prɑ̃ pɑ]

Write it down, please.
Pouvez-vous l'écrire, s'il vous plaît.
[puve vu lekrir, sil vu plɛ]

Okay. Can I pay with a credit card?
D'accord. Puis-je payer avec la carte?
[dakɔ:r. pɥiʒ peje avɛk la kart?]

Yes, you can.
Oui, bien sûr.
[wi, bjɛ̃ sy:r]

Here's your receipt.
Voici votre reçu.
[vwasi vɔtr rəsy]

Sorry about the fine.
Désolé pour l'amende.
[dezɔle pur lamɑ̃:d]

That's okay. It was my fault.
Ça va. C'est de ma faute.
[sa va. sɛ də ma fot]

Enjoy your trip.
Bon voyage.
[bɔ̃ vwaja:ʒ]

Taxi

taxi
taxi
[taksi]

taxi driver
chauffeur de taxi
[ʃofœr də taksi]

to catch a taxi
prendre un taxi
[prɑ̃dr œ̃ taksi]

taxi stand
arrêt de taxi
[arɛ də taksi]

Where can I get a taxi?
Où puis-je trouver un taxi?
[u pɥiʒ truve œ̃ taksi?]

to call a taxi
appeler un taxi
[aple œ̃ taksi]

I need a taxi.
Il me faut un taxi.
[il mə fo œ̃ taksi]

Right now.
maintenant
[mɛ̃tnɑ̃]

What is your address (location)?
Quelle est votre adresse?
[kɛl ɛ vɔtr adrɛs?]

My address is …
Mon adresse est …
[mɔn adrɛs ɛ …]

Your destination?
Votre destination?
[vɔtr dɛstinasjɔ̃?]

Excuse me, …
Excusez-moi, …
[ɛkskyze mwa, …]

Are you available?
Vous êtes libre ?
[vuzɛt libr?]

How much is it to get to …?
Combien ça coûte pour aller à …?
[kɔ̃bjɛ̃ sa kut pur ale a …?]

Do you know where it is?
Vous savez où ça se trouve?
[vu save u sa sə truːv?]

Airport, please.
À l'aéroport, s'il vous plaît.
[a laerɔpɔːr, sil vu plɛ]

Stop here, please.
Arrêtez ici, s'il vous plaît.
[arɛte isi, sil vu plɛ]

It's not here.
Ce n'est pas ici.
[sə nɛ pɑ isi]

This is the wrong address.
C'est la mauvaise adresse.
[sɛ la mɔvɛz adrɛs]

Turn left.
tournez à gauche
[turne a goʃ]

Turn right.
tournez à droite
[turne a drwat]

How much do I owe you?

Combien je vous dois?
[kɔ̃bjɛ̃ ʒə vu dwa?]

I'd like a receipt, please.

**J'aimerais avoir un reçu,
s'il vous plaît.**
[ʒɛmrɛ avwar œ̃ rəsy,
sil vu plɛ]

Keep the change.

Gardez la monnaie.
[garde la mɔnɛ]

Would you please wait for me?

Attendez-moi, s'il vous plaît …
[atɑ̃de-mwa, sil vu plɛ …]

five minutes

cinq minutes
[sɛ̃k minyt]

ten minutes

dix minutes
[di minyt]

fifteen minutes

quinze minutes
[kɛ̃z minyt]

twenty minutes

vingt minutes
[vɛ̃ minyt]

half an hour

une demi-heure
[yn dəmiœr]

Hotel

Hello.	**Bonjour.** [bɔ̃ʒuːr]
My name is ...	**Je m'appelle ...** [ʒə mapɛl ...]
I have a reservation.	**J'ai réservé une chambre.** [ʒe rezɛrve yn ʃɑ̃:br]
I need ...	**Je voudrais ...** [ʒə vudrɛ ...]
a single room	**une chambre simple** [yn ʃɑ̃br sɛ̃pl]
a double room	**une chambre double** [yn ʃɑ̃br dubl]
How much is that?	**C'est combien?** [sɛ kɔ̃bjɛ̃?]
That's a bit expensive.	**C'est un peu cher.** [sɛtœ̃pø ʃɛːr]
Do you have any other options?	**Avez-vous autre chose?** [ave vu otr ʃoːz?]
I'll take it.	**Je vais la prendre.** [ʒə ve la prɑ̃dr]
I'll pay in cash.	**Je vais payer comptant.** [ʒə ve peje kɔ̃tɑ̃]
I've got a problem.	**J'ai un problème.** [ʒe œ̃ prɔblɛm]
My ... is broken.	**... est cassé /cassée/** [... ɛ kɑse]
My ... is out of order.	**... ne fonctionne pas.** [... nə fɔ̃ksjɔn pɑ]
TV	**la télé ...** [la tele ...]
air conditioning	**air conditionné ...** [ɛr kɔ̃disjɔne ...]
tap	**le robinet ...** [lə rɔbinɛ ...]
shower	**ma douche ...** [ma duʃ ...]
sink	**mon évier ...** [mon evje ...]
safe	**mon coffre-fort ...** [mɔ̃ kɔfr-fɔr ...]

door lock	**la serrure de porte …** [la seryr də pɔrt …]
electrical outlet	**la prise électrique …** [la priz elɛktrik …]
hairdryer	**mon sèche-cheveux …** [mɔ̃ sɛʃ ʃəvø …]

I don't have …	**Je n'ai pas …** [ʒə ne pɑ …]
water	**d'eau** [do]
light	**de lumière** [də lymjɛr]
electricity	**d'électricité** [delɛktrisite]

Can you give me …?	**Pouvez-vous me donner …?** [puve vu mə dɔne …?]
a towel	**une serviette** [yn sɛrvjɛt]
a blanket	**une couverture** [yn kuvɛrtyr]
slippers	**des pantoufles** [de pɑ̃tufl]
a robe	**une robe de chambre** [yn rɔb də ʃɑ̃br]
shampoo	**du shampooing** [dy ʃɑ̃pwɛ̃]
soap	**du savon** [dy savɔ̃]

I'd like to change rooms.	**Je voudrais changer ma chambre.** [ʒə vudrɛ ʃɑ̃ʒe ma ʃɑ̃:br]
I can't find my key.	**Je ne trouve pas ma clé.** [ʒə nə truv pɑ ma kle]
Could you open my room, please?	**Pourriez-vous ouvrir ma chambre, s'il vous plaît?** [purje-vu uvrir ma ʃɑ̃:br, sil vu plɛ?]
Who's there?	**Qui est là?** [ki ɛ la?]
Come in!	**Entrez!** [ɑ̃tre!]
Just a minute!	**Une minute!** [yn minyt!]

Not right now, please.	**Pas maintenant, s'il vous plaît.** [pɑ mɛ̃tnɑ̃, sil vu plɛ]
Come to my room, please.	**Pouvez-vous venir à ma chambre, s'il vous plaît.** [puve vu vənir a ma ʃɑ̃:br, sil vu plɛ]

I'd like to order food service.	**J'aimerais avoir le service d'étage.** [ʒɛmrɛ avwar lə sɛrvis deta:ʒ]
My room number is …	**Mon numéro de chambre est le …** [mɔ̃ nymero də ʃɑ̃br ɛ lə …]

I'm leaving …	**Je pars …** [ʒə par …]
We're leaving …	**Nous partons …** [nu partɔ̃ …]
right now	**maintenant** [mɛ̃tnɑ̃]
this afternoon	**cet après-midi** [sɛt aprɛmidi]
tonight	**ce soir** [sə swar]
tomorrow	**demain** [dəmɛ̃]
tomorrow morning	**demain matin** [dəmɛ̃ matɛ̃]
tomorrow evening	**demain après-midi** [dəmɛ̃ aprɛmidi]
the day after tomorrow	**après-demain** [aprɛdmɛ̃]

I'd like to pay.	**Je voudrais régler mon compte.** [ʒə vudrɛ regle mɔ̃ kɔ̃:t]
Everything was wonderful.	**Tout était merveilleux.** [tutetɛ mɛrvɛjø]
Where can I get a taxi?	**Où puis-je trouver un taxi?** [u pɥiʒ truve œ̃ taksi?]
Would you call a taxi for me, please?	**Pourriez-vous m'appeler un taxi, s'il vous plaît?** [purje-vu maple œ̃ taksi, sil vu plɛ?]

Restaurant

Can I look at the menu, please?	**Puis-je voir le menu, s'il vous plaît?** [pɥiʒ vwar lə məny, sil vu plɛ?]
Table for one.	**Une table pour une personne.** [yn tabl pur yn pɛrsɔn]
There are two (three, four) of us.	**Nous sommes deux (trois, quatre).** [nu sɔm dø (trwa, katr)]
Smoking	**Fumeurs** [fymœr]
No smoking	**Non-fumeurs** [nɔ̃-fymœr]
Excuse me! (addressing a waiter)	**S'il vous plaît!** [sil vu plɛ!]
menu	**menu** [məny]
wine list	**carte des vins** [kart de vɛ̃]
The menu, please.	**Le menu, s'il vous plaît.** [lə məny, sil vu plɛ]
Are you ready to order?	**Êtes-vous prêts à commander?** [ɛt-vu prɛ a kɔmɑ̃de?]
What will you have?	**Qu'allez-vous prendre?** [kale-vu prɑ̃dr?]
I'll have ...	**Je vais prendre ...** [ʒə ve prɑ̃dr ...]
I'm a vegetarian.	**Je suis végétarien.** [ʒə sɥi veʒetarjɛ̃]
meat	**viande** [vjɑ̃d]
fish	**poisson** [pwasɔ̃]
vegetables	**légumes** [legym]
Do you have vegetarian dishes?	**Avez-vous des plats végétariens?** [ave vu de pla veʒetarjɛ̃?]
I don't eat pork.	**Je ne mange pas de porc.** [ʒə nə mɑ̃ʒ pa də pɔ:r]
He /she/ doesn't eat meat.	**Il /elle/ ne mange pas de viande.** [il /ɛl/ nə mɑ̃ʒ pa də vjɑ̃:d]
I am allergic to ...	**Je suis allergique à ...** [ʒə sɥi alɛrʒik a ...]

Would you please bring me ...

**Pourriez-vous m'apporter ...,
s'il vous plaît.**
[purje-vu mapɔrte ... ,
sil vu plɛ]

salt | pepper | sugar

le sel | le poivre | du sucre
[lə sɛl | lə pwavr | dy sykr]

coffee | tea | dessert

un café | un thé | un dessert
[œ̃ kafe | œ̃ te | œ̃ desɛr]

water | sparkling | plain

de l'eau | gazeuse | plate
[də lo | gɑzøz | plat]

a spoon | fork | knife

**une cuillère | une fourchette |
un couteau**
[yn kɥijɛr | yn furʃɛt |
œ̃ kuto]

a plate | napkin

une assiette | une serviette
[yn asjɛt | yn sɛrvjɛt]

Enjoy your meal!

Bon appétit!
[bɔn apeti!]

One more, please.

Un de plus, s'il vous plaît.
[œ̃ də plys, sil vu plɛ]

It was very delicious.

C'était délicieux.
[setɛ delisjø]

check | change | tip

**l'addition | de la monnaie |
le pourboire**
[ladisjɔ̃ | də la mɔnɛ | lə purbwar]

Check, please.
(Could I have the check, please?)

L'addition, s'il vous plaît.
[ladisjɔ̃, sil vu plɛ]

Can I pay by credit card?

Puis-je payer avec la carte?
[pɥiʒ peje avɛk la kart?]

I'm sorry, there's a mistake here.

**Excusez-moi, je crois qu'il y a une
erreur ici.**
[ɛkskyze mwa, ʒə krwa kilja yn
ɛrœr isi]

Shopping

Can I help you?
Est-ce que je peux vous aider?
[ɛskə ʒə pø vuzɛde?]

Do you have ...?
Avez-vous ... ?
[ave vu ...?]

I'm looking for ...
Je cherche ...
[ʒə ʃɛrʃ ...]

I need ...
Il me faut ...
[il mə fo ...]

I'm just looking.
Je regarde seulement, merci.
[ʒə rəgard sœlmã, mɛrsi]

We're just looking.
Nous regardons seulement, merci.
[nu rəgardõ sœlmã, mɛrsi]

I'll come back later.
Je reviendrai plus tard.
[ʒə rəvjɛ̃dre ply ta:r]

We'll come back later.
On reviendra plus tard.
[õ rəvjɛ̃dra ply ta:r]

discounts | sale
Rabais | Soldes
[rabɛ | sɔld]

Would you please show me ...
Montrez-moi, s'il vous plaît ...
[mõtre-mwa, sil vu plɛ ...]

Would you please give me ...
Donnez-moi, s'il vous plaît ...
[dɔne-mwa, sil vu plɛ ...]

Can I try it on?
Est-ce que je peux l'essayer?
[ɛskə ʒə pø lesɛje?]

Excuse me, where's the fitting room?
Excusez-moi, où est la cabine d'essayage?
[ɛkskyze mwa, u ɛ la kabin desɛja:ʒ?]

Which color would you like?
Quelle couleur aimeriez-vous?
[kɛl kulœr ɛmərje-vu?]

size | length
taille | longueur
[taj | lõgœr]

How does it fit?
Est-ce que la taille convient ?
[ɛskə la taj kõvjɛ̃?]

How much is it?
Combien ça coûte?
[kõbjɛ̃ sa kut?]

That's too expensive.
C'est trop cher.
[sɛ tro ʃɛ:r]

I'll take it.
Je vais le prendre.
[ʒə ve lə prãdr]

Excuse me, where do I pay?

Excusez-moi, où est la caisse?
[ɛkskyze mwa, u ɛ la kɛs?]

Will you pay in cash or credit card?

Payerez-vous comptant ou par carte de crédit?
[pɛjre-vu kõtã u par kart də kredi?]

In cash | with credit card

Comptant | par carte de crédit
[kõtã | par kart də kredi]

Do you want the receipt?

Voulez-vous un reçu?
[vule vu œ̃ rəsy?]

Yes, please.

Oui, s'il vous plaît.
[wi, sil vu plɛ]

No, it's OK.

Non, ce n'est pas nécessaire.
[nõ, sə nɛ pɑ nesesɛ:r]

Thank you. Have a nice day!

Merci. Bonne journée!
[mɛrsi. bɔn ʒurne!]

In town

Excuse me, please.	**Excusez-moi, ...** [ɛkskyze mwa, ...]
I'm looking for ...	**Je cherche ...** [ʒə ʃɛrʃ ...]
the subway	**le métro** [lə metro]
my hotel	**mon hôtel** [mɔn otɛl]
the movie theater	**le cinéma** [lə sinema]
a taxi stand	**un arrêt de taxi** [œn arɛ də taksi]
an ATM	**un distributeur** [œ̃ distribytœːr]
a foreign exchange office	**un bureau de change** [œ̃ byro də ʃɑ̃ʒ]
an internet café	**un café internet** [œ̃ kafe ɛ̃tɛrnɛt]
... street	**la rue ...** [la ry ...]
this place	**cette place-ci** [sɛt plas-si]
Do you know where ... is?	**Savez-vous où se trouve ...?** [save vu u sə truv ...?]
Which street is this?	**Quelle est cette rue?** [kɛl ɛ sɛt ry?]
Show me where we are right now.	**Montrez-moi où sommes-nous, s'il vous plaît.** [mɔ̃tre-mwa u sɔm-nu, sil vu plɛ]
Can I get there on foot?	**Est-ce que je peux y aller à pied?** [ɛskə ʒə pø i ale a pje?]
Do you have a map of the city?	**Avez-vous une carte de la ville?** [ave vu yn kart də la vil?]
How much is a ticket to get in?	**C'est combien pour un ticket?** [sɛ kɔ̃bjɛ̃ pur œ̃ tikɛ?]
Can I take pictures here?	**Est-ce que je peux faire des photos?** [ɛskə ʒə pø fɛr de foto?]
Are you open?	**Êtes-vous ouvert?** [ɛt-vu uvɛːr?]

When do you open?

À quelle heure ouvrez-vous?
[a kɛl œr uvre-vu?]

When do you close?

À quelle heure fermez-vous?
[a kɛl œr fɛrme-vu?]

Money

money	**argent** [arʒɑ̃]
cash	**argent liquide** [arʒɑ̃ likid]
paper money	**des billets** [de bijɛ]
loose change	**petite monnaie** [pətit mɔnɛ]
check | change | tip	**l'addition | de la monnaie |** **le pourboire** [ladisjɔ̃ | də la mɔnɛ | lə purbwar]
credit card	**carte de crédit** [kart də kredi]
wallet	**portefeuille** [pɔrtəfœj]
to buy	**acheter** [aʃte]
to pay	**payer** [peje]
fine	**amende** [amɑ̃d]
free	**gratuit** [gratɥi]
Where can I buy ...?	**Où puis-je acheter ... ?** [u pɥiʒ aʃte ...?]
Is the bank open now?	**Est-ce que la banque est ouverte** **en ce moment?** [ɛskə la bɑ̃k ɛtuvɛrt ɑ̃ sə mɔmɑ̃?]
When does it open?	**À quelle heure ouvre-t-elle?** [a kɛl œr uvr-tɛl?]
When does it close?	**À quelle heure ferme-t-elle?** [a kɛl œr fɛrm-tɛl?]
How much?	**C'est combien?** [sɛ kɔ̃bjɛ̃?]
How much is this?	**Combien ça coûte?** [kɔ̃bjɛ̃ sa kut?]
That's too expensive.	**C'est trop cher.** [sɛ tro ʃɛːr]

Excuse me, where do I pay?

Excusez-moi, où est la caisse?
[ɛkskyze mwa, u ɛ la kɛs?]

Check, please.

L'addition, s'il vous plaît.
[ladisjɔ̃, sil vu plɛ]

Can I pay by credit card?

Puis-je payer avec la carte?
[pɥiʒ peje avɛk la kart?]

Is there an ATM here?

Est-ce qu'il y a un distributeur ici?
[ɛskilja œ̃ distribytœːr isi?]

I'm looking for an ATM.

Je cherche un distributeur.
[ʒə ʃɛrʃ œ̃ distribytœːr]

I'm looking for a foreign exchange office.

Je cherche un bureau de change.
[ʒə ʃɛrʃ œ̃ byro də ʃɑ̃ːʒ]

I'd like to change …

Je voudrais changer …
[ʒə vudrɛ ʃɑ̃ʒe …]

What is the exchange rate?

Quel est le taux de change?
[kɛl ɛ lə to də ʃɑ̃ːʒ?]

Do you need my passport?

Avez-vous besoin de mon passeport?
[ave vu bəzwɛ̃ də mɔ̃ paspɔːr?]

Time

What time is it?	**Quelle heure est-il?** [kɛl œr ɛ-til?]
When?	**Quand?** [kɑ̃?]
At what time?	**À quelle heure?** [a kɛl œːr?]
now | later | after …	**maintenant | plus tard | après …** [mɛ̃tnɑ̃ | ply tar | aprɛ …]
one o'clock	**une heure** [yn œːr]
one fifteen	**une heure et quart** [yn œːr e kar]
one thirty	**une heure et demie** [yn œːr e dəmi]
one forty-five	**deux heures moins quart** [døzœr mwɛ̃ kar]
one | two | three	**un | deux | trois** [œ̃ | dø | trwɑ]
four | five | six	**quatre | cinq | six** [katr | sɛ̃k | sis]
seven | eight | nine	**sept | huit | neuf** [sɛt | ɥit | nœf]
ten | eleven | twelve	**dix | onze | douze** [dis | ɔ̃z | duz]
in …	**dans …** [dɑ̃ …]
five minutes	**cinq minutes** [sɛ̃k minyt]
ten minutes	**dix minutes** [di minyt]
fifteen minutes	**quinze minutes** [kɛ̃z minyt]
twenty minutes	**vingt minutes** [vɛ̃ minyt]
half an hour	**une demi-heure** [yn dəmiœr]
an hour	**une heure** [yn œːr]

in the morning	**dans la matinée** [dɑ̃ la matine]
early in the morning	**tôt le matin** [to lə matɛ̃]
this morning	**ce matin** [sə matɛ̃]
tomorrow morning	**demain matin** [dəmɛ̃ matɛ̃]
at noon	**à midi** [a midi]
in the afternoon	**dans l'après-midi** [dɑ̃ laprɛmidi]
in the evening	**dans la soirée** [dɑ̃ la sware]
tonight	**ce soir** [sə swar]
at night	**la nuit** [la nɥi]
yesterday	**hier** [jɛr]
today	**aujourd'hui** [oʒurdɥi]
tomorrow	**demain** [dəmɛ̃]
the day after tomorrow	**après-demain** [aprɛdmɛ̃]
What day is it today?	**Quel jour sommes-nous aujourd'hui?** [kɛl ʒur sɔm-nu oʒurdɥi?]
It's ...	**Nous sommes ...** [nu sɔm ...]
Monday	**lundi** [lœ̃di]
Tuesday	**mardi** [mɑrdi]
Wednesday	**mercredi** [mɛrkrədi]
Thursday	**jeudi** [ʒødi]
Friday	**vendredi** [vɑ̃drədi]
Saturday	**samedi** [samdi]
Sunday	**dimanche** [dimɑ̃ʃ]

Greetings. Introductions

Hello.
Bonjour.
[bõʒu:r]

Pleased to meet you.
Enchanté /Enchantée/
[ãʃãte]

Me too.
Moi aussi.
[mwa osi]

I'd like you to meet ...
Je voudrais vous présenter ...
[ʒə vudrɛ vu prezãte ...]

Nice to meet you.
Ravi /Ravie/ de vous rencontrer.
[ravi də vu rãkõtre.]

How are you?
Comment allez-vous?
[kɔmãtalevu?]

My name is ...
Je m'appelle ...
[ʒə mapɛl ...]

His name is ...
Il s'appelle ...
[il sapɛl ...]

Her name is ...
Elle s'appelle ...
[ɛl sapɛl ...]

What's your name?
Comment vous appelez-vous?
[kɔmã vuzaple-vu?]

What's his name?
Quel est son nom?
[kɛl ɛ sõ nõ?]

What's her name?
Quel est son nom?
[kɛl ɛ sõ nõ?]

What's your last name?
Quel est votre nom de famille?
[kɛl ɛ vɔtr nõ də famij?]

You can call me ...
Vous pouvez m'appeler ...
[vu puve maple ...]

Where are you from?
D'où êtes-vous?
[du ɛt-vu?]

I'm from ...
Je suis de ...
[ʒə sɥi də ...]

What do you do for a living?
Qu'est-ce que vous faites dans la vie?
[kɛs kə vu fɛt dã la vi?]

Who is this?
Qui est-ce?
[ki ɛs?]

Who is he?
Qui est-il?
[ki ɛ-til?]

Who is she?
Qui est-elle?
[ki ɛtɛl?]

Who are they?
Qui sont-ils?
[ki sõ til?]

This is ...

C'est ...
[sɛ ...]

my friend (masc.)

mon ami
[mɔn ami]

my friend (fem.)

mon amie
[mɔn ami]

my husband

mon mari
[mɔ̃ mari]

my wife

ma femme
[ma fam]

---

my father

mon père
[mɔ̃ pɛr]

my mother

ma mère
[ma mɛr]

my brother

mon frère
[mɔ̃ frɛr]

my sister

ma soeur
[ma sœr]

my son

mon fils
[mɔ̃ fis]

my daughter

ma fille
[ma fij]

This is our son.

C'est notre fils.
[sɛ nɔtr fis]

This is our daughter.

C'est notre fille.
[sɛ nɔtr fij]

These are my children.

Ce sont mes enfants.
[sə sɔ̃ mezɑ̃fɑ̃]

These are our children.

Ce sont nos enfants.
[sə sɔ̃ nozɑ̃fɑ̃]

Farewells

Good bye!	**Au revoir!** [o rəvwa:r!]
Bye! (inform.)	**Salut!** [saly!]
See you tomorrow.	**À demain.** [a dəmɛ̃]
See you soon.	**À bientôt.** [a bjɛ̃to]
See you at seven.	**On se revoit à sept heures.** [ɔ̃ sə rəvwa a sɛt œ:r]
Have fun!	**Amusez-vous bien!** [amyze vu bjɛ̃!]
Talk to you later.	**On se voit plus tard.** [ɔ̃ sə vwa ply ta:r]
Have a nice weekend.	**Bonne fin de semaine.** [bɔn fɛ̃ də səmɛn]
Good night.	**Bonne nuit.** [bɔn nɥi]
It's time for me to go.	**Il est l'heure que je parte.** [il ɛ lœr kə ʒə part]
I have to go.	**Je dois m'en aller.** [ʒə dwa mãnale]
I will be right back.	**Je reviens tout de suite.** [ʒə rəvjɛ̃ tu də sɥit]
It's late.	**Il est tard.** [il ɛ ta:r]
I have to get up early.	**Je dois me lever tôt.** [ʒə dwa mə ləve to]
I'm leaving tomorrow.	**Je pars demain.** [ʒə par dəmɛ̃]
We're leaving tomorrow.	**Nous partons demain.** [nu partɔ̃ dəmɛ̃]
Have a nice trip!	**Bon voyage!** [bɔ̃ vwaja:ʒ!]
It was nice meeting you.	**Enchanté de faire votre connaissance.** [ɑ̃ʃɑ̃te də fɛr vɔtr kɔnɛsɑ̃:s]
It was nice talking to you.	**Heureux /Heureuse/ d'avoir parlé avec vous.** [ørø /ørøz/ davwar parle avɛk vu]

Thanks for everything.

Merci pour tout.
[mɛrsi pur tu]

I had a very good time.

Je me suis vraiment amusé /amusée/
[ʒə mə sɥi vrɛmɑ̃ amyze]

We had a very good time.

Nous nous sommes vraiment amusés /amusées/
[nu nu sɔm vrɛmɑ̃ amyze]

It was really great.

C'était vraiment plaisant.
[setɛ vrɛmɑ̃ plɛzɑ̃]

I'm going to miss you.

Vous allez me manquer.
[vuzale mə mɑ̃ke]

We're going to miss you.

Vous allez nous manquer.
[vuzale nu mɑ̃ke]

Good luck!

Bonne chance!
[bɔn ʃɑ̃:s!]

Say hi to …

Mes salutations à …
[me salytasjɔ̃ a …]

Foreign language

I don't understand.	**Je ne comprends pas.** [ʒə nə kɔ̃prɑ̃ pa]
Write it down, please.	**Écrivez-le, s'il vous plaît.** [ekrive lə, sil vu plɛ]
Do you speak …?	**Parlez-vous …?** [parle vu …?]

I speak a little bit of …	**Je parle un peu …** [ʒə parl œ̃ pø …]
English	**anglais** [ɑ̃glɛ]
Turkish	**turc** [tyrk]
Arabic	**arabe** [arab]
French	**français** [frɑ̃sɛ]

German	**allemand** [almɑ̃]
Italian	**italien** [italjɛ̃]
Spanish	**espagnol** [ɛspaɲɔl]
Portuguese	**portugais** [pɔrtygɛ]
Chinese	**chinois** [ʃinwa]
Japanese	**japonais** [ʒaponɛ]

Can you repeat that, please.	**Pouvez-vous le répéter, s'il vous plaît.** [puve vu lə repete, sil vu plɛ]
I understand.	**Je comprends.** [ʒə kɔ̃prɑ̃]
I don't understand.	**Je ne comprends pas.** [ʒə nə kɔ̃prɑ̃ pa]
Please speak more slowly.	**Parlez plus lentement, s'il vous plaît.** [parle ply lɑ̃tmɑ̃, sil vu plɛ]

Is that correct? (Am I saying it right?)	**Est-ce que c'est correct?** [ɛskə sɛ kɔrrɛkt?]
What is this? (What does this mean?)	**Qu'est-ce que c'est?** [kɛskə sɛ?]

Apologies

Excuse me, please.	**Excusez-moi, s'il vous plaît.**
	[ɛkskyze mwa, sil vu plɛ]
I'm sorry.	**Je suis désolé /désolée/**
	[ʒə sɥi dezɔle]
I'm really sorry.	**Je suis vraiment /désolée/**
	[ʒə sɥi vrɛmɑ̃ dezɔle]
Sorry, it's my fault.	**Désolé /Désolée/, c'est ma faute.**
	[dezɔle, sɛ ma fot]
My mistake.	**Au temps pour moi.**
	[otɑ̃ pur mwa]

May I ...?	**Puis-je ... ?**
	[pɥiʒ ...?]
Do you mind if I ...?	**Ça vous dérange si je ...?**
	[sa vu derɑ̃ʒ si ʒə ...?]
It's OK.	**Ce n'est pas grave.**
	[sə nɛ pɑ graːv]
It's all right.	**Ça va.**
	[sa va]
Don't worry about it.	**Ne vous inquiétez pas.**
	[nə vuzɛ̃kjete pɑ]

Agreement

Yes.	**Oui** [wi]
Yes, sure.	**Oui, bien sûr.** [wi, bjɛ̃ sy:r]
OK (Good!)	**Bien.** [bjɛ̃]
Very well.	**Très bien.** [trɛ bjɛ̃]
Certainly!	**Bien sûr!** [bjɛ̃sy:r!]
I agree.	**Je suis d'accord.** [ʒə sɥi dakɔ:r]
That's correct.	**C'est correct.** [sɛ kɔrrɛkt]
That's right.	**C'est exact.** [sɛtɛgzakt]
You're right.	**Vous avez raison.** [vuzave rɛzɔ̃]
I don't mind.	**Je ne suis pas contre.** [ʒə nə sɥi pɑ kɔ̃tr]
Absolutely right.	**Tout à fait correct.** [tutafɛ kɔrrɛkt]
It's possible.	**C'est possible.** [sɛ pɔsibl]
That's a good idea.	**C'est une bonne idée.** [sɛtyn bɔn ide]
I can't say no.	**Je ne peux pas dire non.** [ʒə nə pø pɑ dir nɔ̃]
I'd be happy to.	**J'en serai ravi /ravie/** [ʒɑ̃ səre ravi:]
With pleasure.	**Avec plaisir.** [avɛk plezi:r]

Refusal. Expressing doubt

No.	**Non** [nɔ̃]
Certainly not.	**Absolument pas.** [absɔlymɑ̃ pɑ]
I don't agree.	**Je ne suis pas d'accord.** [ʒə nə sɥi pɑ dakɔ:r]
I don't think so.	**Je ne le crois pas.** [ʒə nə lə krwa pɑ]
It's not true.	**Ce n'est pas vrai.** [sə nɛ pɑ vrɛ]
You are wrong.	**Vous avez tort.** [vuzave tɔ:r]
I think you are wrong.	**Je pense que vous avez tort.** [ʒə pɑ̃s kə vuzave tɔ:r]
I'm not sure.	**Je ne suis pas sûr /sûre/** [ʒə nə sɥi pɑ sy:r]
It's impossible.	**C'est impossible.** [sɛtɛ̃pɔsibl]
Nothing of the kind (sort)!	**Pas du tout!** [pɑ dy tu!]
The exact opposite.	**Au contraire!** [o kɔ̃trɛ:r!]
I'm against it.	**Je suis contre.** [ʒə sɥi kɔ̃tr]
I don't care.	**Ça m'est égal.** [sa mɛ tegal]
I have no idea.	**Je n'ai aucune idée.** [ʒə ne okyn ide]
I doubt that.	**Je doute que cela soit ainsi.** [ʒə dut kə səla swa ɛ̃si]
Sorry, I can't.	**Désolé /Désolée/, je ne peux pas.** [dezɔle, ʒə nə pø pɑ]
Sorry, I don't want to.	**Désolé /Désolée/, je ne veux pas.** [dezɔle, ʒə nə vø pɑ]
Thank you, but I don't need this.	**Merci, mais ça ne m'intéresse pas.** [mɛrsi, mɛ sa nə mɛ̃terɛs pɑ]
It's late.	**Il se fait tard.** [il sə fɛ ta:r]

I have to get up early.

Je dois me lever tôt.
[ʒə dwa mə ləve to]

I don't feel well.

Je ne me sens pas bien.
[ʒə nə mə sɑ̃ pɑ bjɛ̃]

Expressing gratitude

Thank you. — **Merci.**
[mɛrsi]

Thank you very much. — **Merci beaucoup.**
[mɛrsi boku]

I really appreciate it. — **Je l'apprécie beaucoup.**
[ʒə lapresi boku]

I'm really grateful to you. — **Je vous suis très reconnaissant.**
[ʒə vu sɥi trɛ rəkɔnɛsɑ̃]

We are really grateful to you. — **Nous vous sommes très reconnaissant.**
[nu vu sɔm trɛ rəkɔnɛsɑ̃]

Thank you for your time. — **Merci pour votre temps.**
[mɛrsi pur vɔtr tɑ̃]

Thanks for everything. — **Merci pour tout.**
[mɛrsi pur tu]

Thank you for ... — **Merci pour ...**
[mɛrsi pur ...]

your help — **votre aide**
[vɔtr ɛd]

a nice time — **les bons moments passés**
[le bɔ̃ mɔmɑ̃ pase]

a wonderful meal — **un repas merveilleux**
[œ̃ rəpɑ mɛrvɛjø]

a pleasant evening — **cette agréable soirée**
[sɛt agreabl sware]

a wonderful day — **cette merveilleuse journée**
[sɛt mɛrvɛjøz ʒurne]

an amazing journey — **une excursion extraordinaire**
[yn ɛkskyrsjɔ̃ ɛkstraɔrdinɛr]

Don't mention it. — **Il n'y a pas de quoi.**
[il njapɑ də kwa]

You are welcome. — **Je vous en prie.**
[ʒə vuzɑ̃pri]

Any time. — **Mon plaisir.**
[mɔ̃ plezi:r]

My pleasure. — **J'ai été heureux /heureuse/ de vous aider.**
[ʒe ete ørø /ørøz/ də vuzɛde]

Forget it. It's alright.

Ça va. N'y pensez plus.
[sa va. ni pɑ̃se ply]

Don't worry about it.

Ne vous inquiétez pas.
[nə vuzɛ̃kjete pɑ]

Congratulations. Best wishes

Congratulations!	**Félicitations!** [felisitasjɔ̃!]
Happy birthday!	**Joyeux anniversaire!** [ʒwajø zanivɛrsɛ:r!]
Merry Christmas!	**Joyeux Noël!** [ʒwajø nɔɛl!]
Happy New Year!	**Bonne Année!** [bɔn ane!]
Happy Easter!	**Joyeuses Pâques!** [ʒwajøz pɑk!]
Happy Hanukkah!	**Joyeux Hanoukka!** [ʒwajø anuka!]
I'd like to propose a toast.	**Je voudrais proposer un toast.** [ʒə vudrɛ prɔpoze œ̃ tost]
Cheers!	**Santé!** [sɑ̃te!]
Let's drink to …!	**Buvons à …!** [byvɔ̃ a …!]
To our success!	**À notre succès!** [a nɔtr syksɛ!]
To your success!	**À votre succès!** [a vɔtr syksɛ!]
Good luck!	**Bonne chance!** [bɔn ʃɑ̃:s!]
Have a nice day!	**Bonne journée!** [bɔn ʒurne!]
Have a good holiday!	**Passez de bonnes vacances !** [pɑse də bɔn vakɑ̃s!]
Have a safe journey!	**Bon voyage!** [bɔ̃ vwaja:ʒ!]
I hope you get better soon!	**Rétablissez-vous vite.** [retablise-vu vit]

Socializing

Why are you sad?

Pourquoi êtes-vous si triste?
[purkwa ɛt-vu si trist?]

Smile! Cheer up!

Souriez!
[surje!]

Are you free tonight?

Êtes-vous libre ce soir?
[ɛt-vu libr sə swa:r?]

May I offer you a drink?

Puis-je vous offrir un verre?
[pɥiʒ vu zɔfrir œ̃ vɛ:r?]

Would you like to dance?

Voulez-vous danser?
[vule-vu dɑ̃se?]

Let's go to the movies.

Et si on va au cinéma?
[e si ɔ̃va o sinema?]

May I invite you to …?

Puis-je vous inviter …?
[pɥiʒ vu zɛ̃vite …?]

a restaurant

au restaurant
[o rɛstɔrɑ̃]

the movies

au cinéma
[o sinema]

the theater

au théâtre
[o teatr]

go for a walk

pour une promenade
[pur yn prɔmnad]

At what time?

À quelle heure?
[a kɛl œ:r?]

tonight

ce soir
[sə swar]

at six

à six heures
[a siz œ:r]

at seven

à sept heures
[a sɛt œ:r]

at eight

à huit heures
[a ɥit œ:r]

at nine

à neuf heures
[a nœv œ:r]

Do you like it here?

Est-ce que vous aimez cet endroit?
[ɛskə vuzɛme sɛt ɑ̃drwa?]

Are you here with someone?

Êtes-vous ici avec quelqu'un?
[ɛt-vu isi avɛk kelkœ̃?]

I'm with my friend.

Je suis avec mon ami.
[ʒə sɥi avɛk mɔn ami]

I'm with my friends.	**Je suis avec mes amis.** [ʒə sɥi avɛk mezami]
No, I'm alone.	**Non, je suis seul /seule/** [nɔ̃, ʒə sɥi sœl]

Do you have a boyfriend?	**As-tu un copain?** [a ty œ̃ kɔpɛ̃?]
I have a boyfriend.	**J'ai un copain.** [ʒe œ̃ kɔpɛ̃]
Do you have a girlfriend?	**As-tu une copine?** [a ty yn kɔpin?]
I have a girlfriend.	**J'ai une copine.** [ʒe yn kɔpin]

Can I see you again?	**Est-ce que je peux te revoir?** [ɛskə ʒə pø tə rəvwa:r?]
Can I call you?	**Est-ce que je peux t'appeler?** [ɛskə ʒə pø taple?]
Call me. (Give me a call.)	**Appelle-moi.** [apɛl mwa]
What's your number?	**Quel est ton numéro?** [kɛl ɛ tɔ̃ nymero?]
I miss you.	**Tu me manques.** [ty mə mɑ̃:k]

You have a beautiful name.	**Vous avez un très beau nom.** [vuzave œ̃ trɛ bo nɔ̃]
I love you.	**Je t'aime.** [ʒə tɛm]
Will you marry me?	**Veux-tu te marier avec moi?** [vø-ty tə marje avɛk mwa?]
You're kidding!	**Vous plaisantez!** [vu plɛzɑ̃te!]
I'm just kidding.	**Je plaisante.** [ʒə plɛzɑ̃:t]

Are you serious?	**Êtes-vous sérieux /sérieuse/?** [ɛt-vu serjø /serjøz/?]
I'm serious.	**Je suis sérieux /sérieuse/** [ʒə sɥi serjø /serjøz/]
Really?!	**Vraiment?!** [vrɛmɑ̃?!]
It's unbelievable!	**C'est incroyable!** [sɛtɛ̃krwajabl!]
I don't believe you.	**Je ne vous crois pas.** [ʒə nə vu krwa pɑ]
I can't.	**Je ne peux pas.** [ʒə nə pø pɑ]
I don't know.	**Je ne sais pas.** [ʒə nə sɛ pɑ]
I don't understand you.	**Je ne vous comprends pas** [ʒə nə vu kɔ̃prɑ̃ pɑ]

Please go away.

Laissez-moi! Allez-vous-en!
[lɛse-mwa! ale-vuzɑ̃!]

Leave me alone!

Laissez-moi tranquille!
[lɛse-mwa trɑ̃kil!]

I can't stand him.

Je ne le supporte pas.
[ʒə nə lə sypɔrt pɑ]

You are disgusting!

Vous êtes dégoûtant!
[vuzɛt degutɑ̃!]

I'll call the police!

Je vais appeler la police!
[ʒə ve aple la pɔlis!]

Sharing impressions. Emotions

I like it.	**J'aime ça.** [ʒɛm sa]
Very nice.	**C'est gentil.** [sɛ ʒɑ̃ti]
That's great!	**C'est super!** [sɛ sypɛr!]
It's not bad.	**C'est assez bien.** [sɛtase bjɛ̃]

I don't like it.	**Je n'aime pas ça.** [ʒə nɛm pɑ sa]
It's not good.	**Ce n'est pas bien.** [sə nɛ pɑ bjɛ̃]
It's bad.	**C'est mauvais.** [sɛ mɔvɛ]
It's very bad.	**Ce n'est pas bien du tout.** [sə nɛ pɑ bjɛ̃ dy tu]
It's disgusting.	**C'est dégoûtant.** [sɛ degutɑ̃]

I'm happy.	**Je suis content /contente/** [ʒə sɥi kɔ̃tɑ̃ /kɔ̃tɑ̃t/]
I'm content.	**Je suis heureux /heureuse/** [ʒə sɥi ørø /ørøz/]
I'm in love.	**Je suis amoureux /amoureuse/** [ʒə sɥi amurø /amurøz/]
I'm calm.	**Je suis calme.** [ʒə sɥi kalm]
I'm bored.	**Je m'ennuie.** [ʒə mɑ̃nɥi]

I'm tired.	**Je suis fatigué /fatiguée/** [ʒə sɥi fatige]
I'm sad.	**Je suis triste.** [ʒə sɥi trist]
I'm frightened.	**J'ai peur.** [ʒə pœ:r]

I'm angry.	**Je suis fâché /fâchée/** [ʒə sɥi faʃe]
I'm worried.	**Je suis inquiet /inquiète/** [ʒə sɥi ɛ̃kjɛ /ɛ̃kjɛt/]
I'm nervous.	**Je suis nerveux /nerveuse/** [ʒə sɥi nɛrvø /nɛrvøz/]

I'm jealous. (envious)

Je suis jaloux /jalouse/
[ʒə sɥi ʒalu /ʒaluz/]

I'm surprised.

Je suis surpris /surprise/
[ʒə sɥi syrpri /syrpriz/]

I'm perplexed.

Je suis gêné /gênée/
[ʒə sɥi ʒɛne]

Problems. Accidents

I've got a problem.

J'ai un problème.
[ʒe œ̃ prɔblɛm]

We've got a problem.

Nous avons un problème.
[nuzavɔ̃ œ̃ prɔblɛm]

I'm lost.

Je suis perdu /perdue/
[ʒə sɥi pɛrdy]

I missed the last bus (train).

J'ai manqué le dernier bus (train).
[ʒe mãke lə dɛrnje bys (trɛ̃)]

I don't have any money left.

Je n'ai plus d'argent.
[ʒə ne ply darʒã]

I've lost my ...

J'ai perdu mon ...
[ʒe pɛrdy mɔ̃ ...]

Someone stole my ...

On m'a volé mon ...
[ɔ̃ ma vɔle mɔ̃ ...]

passport

passeport
[paspɔːr]

wallet

portefeuille
[pɔrtəfœj]

papers

papiers
[papje]

ticket

billet
[bijɛ]

money

argent
[arʒã]

handbag

sac à main
[sak a mɛ̃]

camera

appareil photo
[aparɛj fɔto]

laptop

portable
[pɔrtabl]

tablet computer

ma tablette
[ma tablɛt]

mobile phone

mobile
[mɔbil]

Help me!

Au secours!
[o səkuːr!]

What's happened?

Qu'est-il arrivé?
[kɛtil arive?]

fire

un incendie
[œn ɛ̃sãdi]

shooting	**des coups de feu** [de ku də fø]
murder	**un meurtre** [œ̃ mœrtr]
explosion	**une explosion** [yn ɛksplozjɔ̃]
fight	**une bagarre** [yn bagar]

Call the police!	**Appelez la police!** [aple la polis!]
Please hurry up!	**Dépêchez-vous, s'il vous plaît!** [depɛʃe-vu, sil vu plɛ!]
I'm looking for the police station.	**Je cherche le commissariat de police.** [ʒə ʃɛrʃ lə kɔmisarja də polis]
I need to make a call.	**Il me faut faire un appel.** [il mə fo fɛr œn apɛl]
May I use your phone?	**Puis-je utiliser votre téléphone?** [pɥiʒ ytilize vɔtr telefɔn?]

I've been ...	**J'ai été ...** [ʒe ete ...]
mugged	**agressé /agressée/** [agrɛse]
robbed	**volé /volée/** [vɔle]
raped	**violée** [vjɔle]
attacked (beaten up)	**attaqué /attaquée/** [atake]

Are you all right?	**Est-ce que ça va?** [ɛskə sa va?]
Did you see who it was?	**Avez-vous vu qui c'était?** [ave vu vy ki setɛ?]
Would you be able to recognize the person?	**Pourriez-vous reconnaître cette personne?** [purje-vu rəkɔnɛtr sɛt pɛrsɔn?]
Are you sure?	**Vous êtes sûr?** [vuzɛt syːr?]

Please calm down.	**Calmez-vous, s'il vous plaît.** [kalme-vu, sil vu plɛ]
Take it easy!	**Calmez-vous!** [kalme-vu!]
Don't worry!	**Ne vous inquiétez pas.** [nə vuzɛ̃kjete pɑ]
Everything will be fine.	**Tout ira bien.** [tutira bjɛ̃]
Everything's all right.	**Ça va. Tout va bien.** [sa va. tu va bjɛ̃]

Come here, please.

Venez ici, s'il vous plaît.
[vəne isi, sil vu plɛ]

I have some questions for you.

J'ai des questions à vous poser.
[ʒe de kɛstjõ a vu poze]

Wait a moment, please.

Attendez un moment, s'il vous plaît.
[atãde œ̃ mɔmã, sil vu plɛ]

Do you have any I.D.?

Avez-vous une carte d'identité?
[ave vu yn kart didãtite?]

Thanks. You can leave now.

Merci. Vous pouvez partir maintenant.
[mɛrsi. vu puve partir mɛ̃tnã]

Hands behind your head!

Les mains derrière la tête!
[le mɛ̃ dɛrjɛr la tɛt!]

You're under arrest!

Vous êtes arrêté!
[vuzɛt arɛte!]

Health problems

Please help me.	**Aidez-moi, s'il vous plaît.** [ɛde-mwa, sil vu plɛ]
I don't feel well.	**Je ne me sens pas bien.** [ʒə nə mə sɑ̃ pɑ bjɛ̃]
My husband doesn't feel well.	**Mon mari ne se sent pas bien.** [mɔ̃ mari nə sə sɑ̃ pɑ bjɛ̃]
My son …	**Mon fils …** [mɔ̃ fis …]
My father …	**Mon père …** [mɔ̃ pɛr …]
My wife doesn't feel well.	**Ma femme ne se sent pas bien.** [ma fam nə sə sɑ̃ pɑ bjɛ̃]
My daughter …	**Ma fille …** [ma fij …]
My mother …	**Ma mère …** [ma mɛr …]
I've got a …	**J'ai mal …** [ʒe mal …]
headache	**à la tête** [a la tɛt]
sore throat	**à la gorge** [a la gɔrʒ]
stomach ache	**à l'estomac** [a lɛstɔma]
toothache	**aux dents** [o dɑ̃]
I feel dizzy.	**J'ai le vertige.** [ʒe lə vɛrti:ʒ]
He has a fever.	**Il a de la fièvre.** [il a də la fjɛ:vr]
She has a fever.	**Elle a de la fièvre.** [ɛl a də la fjɛ:vr]
I can't breathe.	**Je ne peux pas respirer.** [ʒə nə pø pɑ rɛspire]
I'm short of breath.	**J'ai du mal à respirer.** [ʒe dy mal a rɛspire]
I am asthmatic.	**Je suis asthmatique.** [ʒə sɥi asmatik]
I am diabetic.	**Je suis diabétique.** [ʒə sɥi djabetik]

I can't sleep.

Je ne peux pas dormir.
[ʒə nə pø pɑ dɔrmiːr]

food poisoning

intoxication alimentaire
[ɛ̃tɔksikasjɔ̃ alimɑ̃tɛr]

It hurts here.

Ça fait mal ici.
[sa fɛ mal isi]

Help me!

Aidez-moi!
[ɛde-mwa!]

I am here!

Je suis ici!
[ʒə sɥi isi!]

We are here!

Nous sommes ici!
[nu sɔm isi!]

Get me out of here!

Sortez-moi d'ici!
[sɔrte mwa disi!]

I need a doctor.

J'ai besoin d'un docteur.
[ʒe bəzwɛ̃ dœ̃ dɔktœːr]

I can't move.

Je ne peux pas bouger!
[ʒə nə pø pɑ buʒe!]

I can't move my legs.

Je ne peux pas bouger mes jambes.
[ʒə nə pø pɑ buʒe me ʒɑ̃ːb]

I have a wound.

Je suis blessé /blessée/
[ʒə sɥi blɛse]

Is it serious?

Est-ce que c'est sérieux?
[ɛskə sɛ serjø?]

My documents are in my pocket.

Mes papiers sont dans ma poche.
[me papje sɔ̃ dɑ̃ ma pɔʃ]

Calm down!

Calmez-vous!
[kalme vu!]

May I use your phone?

Puis-je utiliser votre téléphone?
[pɥiʒ ytilize vɔtr telefɔn?]

Call an ambulance!

Appelez une ambulance!
[aple yn ɑ̃bylɑ̃ːs!]

It's urgent!

C'est urgent!
[sɛtyrʒɑ̃!]

It's an emergency!

C'est une urgence!
[sɛtyn yrʒɑ̃ːs!]

Please hurry up!

Dépêchez-vous, s'il vous plaît!
[depɛʃe-vu, sil vu plɛ!]

Would you please call a doctor?

Appelez le docteur, s'il vous plaît.
[aple lə dɔktœːr, sil vu plɛ]

Where is the hospital?

Où est l'hôpital?
[u ɛ lɔpital?]

How are you feeling?

Comment vous sentez-vous?
[kɔmɑ̃ vu sɑ̃te-vu?]

Are you all right?

Est-ce que ça va?
[ɛskə sa va?]

What's happened?

Qu'est-il arrivé?
[kɛtil arive?]

I feel better now.　　　　　　　　**Je me sens mieux maintenant.**
[ʒə mə sɑ̃ mjø mɛ̃tnɑ̃]

It's OK.　　　　　　　　　　　　**Ça va. Tout va bien.**
[sa va. tu va bjɛ̃]

It's all right.　　　　　　　　　　**Ça va.**
[sa va]

At the pharmacy

pharmacy (drugstore)	**pharmacie** [farmasi]
24-hour pharmacy	**pharmacie 24 heures** [farmasi vɛ̃katr œr]
Where is the closest pharmacy?	**Où se trouve la pharmacie** **la plus proche?** [u sə truv la farmasi la ply prɔʃ?]

Is it open now?	**Est-elle ouverte en ce moment?** [ɛtɛl uvɛrt ɑ̃ sə mɔmɑ̃?]
At what time does it open?	**À quelle heure ouvre-t-elle?** [a kɛl œr uvr tɛl?]
At what time does it close?	**à quelle heure ferme-t-elle?** [a kɛl œr fɛrm tɛl?]

Is it far?	**C'est loin?** [sɛ lwɛ̃?]
Can I get there on foot?	**Est-ce que je peux y aller à pied?** [ɛskə ʒə pø i ale a pje?]
Can you show me on the map?	**Pouvez-vous me le montrer** **sur la carte?** [puve vu mə lə mõtre syr la kart?]

Please give me something for ...	**Pouvez-vous me donner** **quelque chose contre ...** [puve vu mə dɔne kɛlkə ʃoz kõtr ...]
a headache	**le mal de tête** [lə mal də tɛt]
a cough	**la toux** [la tu]
a cold	**le rhume** [lə rym]
the flu	**la grippe** [la grip]

a fever	**la fièvre** [la fjɛ:vr]
a stomach ache	**un mal d'estomac** [œ̃ mal dɛstɔma]
nausea	**la nausée** [la noze]

diarrhea	**la diarrhée** [la djare]
constipation	**la constipation** [la kõstipasjõ]

pain in the back	**un mal de dos** [œ̃ mal də do]
chest pain	**les douleurs de poitrine** [le dulœr də pwatrin]
side stitch	**les points de côté** [le pwɛ̃ də kote]
abdominal pain	**les douleurs abdominales** [le dulœr abdɔminal]

pill	**une pilule** [yn pilyl]
ointment, cream	**un onguent, une crème** [œn õgɑ̃, yn krɛm]
syrup	**un sirop** [œ̃ siro]
spray	**un spray** [œ̃ sprɛ]
drops	**les gouttes** [le gut]

You need to go to the hospital.	**Vous devez allez à l'hôpital.** [vu dəve ale a lɔpital]
health insurance	**assurance maladie** [asyrɑ̃s maladi]
prescription	**prescription** [prɛskripsjõ]
insect repellant	**produit anti-insecte** [prɔdɥi ɑ̃ti-ɛ̃sɛkt]
Band Aid	**bandages adhésifs** [bɑ̃daʒ adezif]

The bare minimum

Excuse me, ...	**Excusez-moi, ...** [ɛkskyze mwa, ...]
Hello.	**Bonjour** [bɔ̃ʒuːr]
Thank you.	**Merci** [mɛrsi]
Good bye.	**Au revoir** [o rəvwaːr]
Yes.	**Oui** [wi]
No.	**Non** [nɔ̃]
I don't know.	**Je ne sais pas.** [ʒə nə sɛ pɑ]
Where? | Where to? | When?	**Où? | Où? | Quand?** [u? | u? | kɑ̃?]
I need ...	**J'ai besoin de ...** [ʒe bəzwɛ̃ də ...]
I want ...	**Je veux ...** [ʒə vø ...]
Do you have ...?	**Avez-vous ... ?** [ave vu ...?]
Is there a ... here?	**Est-ce qu'il y a ... ici?** [ɛs kilja ... isi?]
May I ...?	**Puis-je ... ?** [pɥiʒ ...?]
..., please (polite request)	**..., s'il vous plaît** [..., sil vu plɛ]
I'm looking for ...	**Je cherche ...** [ʒə ʃɛrʃ ...]
restroom	**les toilettes** [le twalɛt]
ATM	**un distributeur** [œ̃ distribytœːr]
pharmacy (drugstore)	**une pharmacie** [yn farmasi]
hospital	**l'hôpital** [lɔpital]
police station	**le commissariat de police** [lə kɔmisarja də polis]
subway	**une station de métro** [yn stasjɔ̃ də metro]

taxi

un taxi
[œ̃ taksi]

train station

la gare
[la gar]

My name is ...

Je m'appelle ...
[ʒə mapɛl ...]

What's your name?

Comment vous appelez-vous?
[kɔmɑ̃ vuzaple-vu?]

Could you please help me?

Aidez-moi, s'il vous plaît.
[ɛde-mwa, sil vu plɛ]

I've got a problem.

J'ai un problème.
[ʒe œ̃ prɔblɛm]

I don't feel well.

Je ne me sens pas bien.
[ʒə nə mə sɑ̃ pɑ bjɛ̃]

Call an ambulance!

Appelez une ambulance!
[aple yn ɑ̃bylɑ̃:s!]

May I make a call?

Puis-je faire un appel?
[pɥiʒ fɛr œn apɛl?]

I'm sorry.

Excusez-moi.
[ɛkskyze mwa]

You're welcome.

Je vous en prie.
[ʒə vuzɑ̃pri]

I, me

je, moi
[ʒə, mwa]

you (inform.)

tu, toi
[ty, twa]

he

il
[il]

she

elle
[ɛl]

they (masc.)

ils
[il]

they (fem.)

elles
[ɛl]

we

nous
[nu]

you (pl)

vous
[vu]

you (sg, form.)

Vous
[vu]

ENTRANCE

ENTRÉE
[ɑ̃tre]

EXIT

SORTIE
[sɔrti]

OUT OF ORDER

HORS SERVICE | EN PANNE
[ɔr sɛrvis | ɑ̃ pan]

CLOSED

FERMÉ
[fɛrme]

OPEN

OUVERT
[uvɛr]

FOR WOMEN

POUR LES FEMMES
[pur le fam]

FOR MEN

POUR LES HOMMES
[pur le zɔm]

T&P BOOKS

MINI DICTIONARY

This section contains 250 useful words required for everyday communication. You will find the names of months and days of the week here. The dictionary also contains topics such as colors, measurements, family, and more

T&P Books Publishing

DICTIONARY CONTENTS

T&P Books Publishing

1. Time. Calendar

time	**temps** (m)	[tɑ̃]
hour	**heure** (f)	[œr]
half an hour	**demi-heure** (f)	[dəmijœr]
minute	**minute** (f)	[minyt]
second	**seconde** (f)	[səgɔ̃d]
today (adv)	**aujourd'hui** (adv)	[oʒurdɥi]
tomorrow (adv)	**demain** (adv)	[dəmɛ̃]
yesterday (adv)	**hier** (adv)	[ijɛr]
Monday	**lundi** (m)	[lœ̃di]
Tuesday	**mardi** (m)	[mardi]
Wednesday	**mercredi** (m)	[mɛrkrədi]
Thursday	**jeudi** (m)	[ʒødi]
Friday	**vendredi** (m)	[vɑ̃drədi]
Saturday	**samedi** (m)	[samdi]
Sunday	**dimanche** (m)	[dimɑ̃ʃ]
day	**jour** (m)	[ʒur]
working day	**jour** (m) **ouvrable**	[ʒur uvrabl]
public holiday	**jour** (m) **férié**	[ʒur ferje]
weekend	**week-end** (m)	[wikɛnd]
week	**semaine** (f)	[səmɛn]
last week (adv)	**la semaine dernière**	[la səmɛn dɛrnjɛr]
next week (adv)	**la semaine prochaine**	[la səmɛn prɔʃɛn]
in the morning	**le matin**	[lə matɛ̃]
in the afternoon	**dans l'après-midi**	[dɑ̃ laprɛmidi]
in the evening	**le soir**	[lə swar]
tonight (this evening)	**ce soir**	[sə swar]
at night	**la nuit**	[la nɥi]
midnight	**minuit** (f)	[minɥi]
January	**janvier** (m)	[ʒɑ̃vje]
February	**février** (m)	[fevrije]
March	**mars** (m)	[mars]
April	**avril** (m)	[avril]
May	**mai** (m)	[mɛ]
June	**juin** (m)	[ʒɥɛ̃]
July	**juillet** (m)	[ʒɥijɛ]
August	**août** (m)	[ut]

September	septembre (m)	[separemɑ̃]
October	octobre (m)	[ɔktɔbr]
November	novembre (m)	[nɔvɑ̃br]
December	décembre (m)	[desɑ̃br]

in spring	au printemps	[oprɛ̃tɑ̃]
in summer	en été	[ɑn ete]
in fall	en automne	[ɑn otɔn]
in winter	en hiver	[ɑn ivɛr]

month	mois (m)	[mwa]
season (summer, etc.)	saison (f)	[sɛzɔ̃]
year	année (f)	[ane]

2. Numbers. Numerals

0 zero	zéro	[zero]
1 one	un	[œ̃]
2 two	deux	[dø]
3 three	trois	[trwa]
4 four	quatre	[katr]

5 five	cinq	[sɛ̃k]
6 six	six	[sis]
7 seven	sept	[sɛt]
8 eight	huit	[ɥit]
9 nine	neuf	[nœf]
10 ten	dix	[dis]

11 eleven	onze	[ɔ̃z]
12 twelve	douze	[duz]
13 thirteen	treize	[trɛz]
14 fourteen	quatorze	[katɔrz]
15 fifteen	quinze	[kɛ̃z]

16 sixteen	seize	[sɛz]
17 seventeen	dix-sept	[disɛt]
18 eighteen	dix-huit	[dizɥit]
19 nineteen	dix-neuf	[diznœf]

20 twenty	vingt	[vɛ̃]
30 thirty	trente	[trɑ̃t]
40 forty	quarante	[karɑ̃t]
50 fifty	cinquante	[sɛ̃kɑ̃t]

60 sixty	soixante	[swasɑ̃t]
70 seventy	soixante-dix	[swasɑ̃tdis]
80 eighty	quatre-vingts	[katrəvɛ̃]
90 ninety	quatre-vingt-dix	[katrəvɛ̃dis]
100 one hundred	cent	[sɑ̃]

200 two hundred	**deux cents**	[dø sɑ̃]
300 three hundred	**trois cents**	[trwa sɑ̃]
400 four hundred	**quatre cents**	[katr sɑ̃]
500 five hundred	**cinq cents**	[sɛ̃k sɑ̃]
600 six hundred	**six cents**	[si sɑ̃]
700 seven hundred	**sept cents**	[sɛt sɑ̃]
800 eight hundred	**huit cents**	[ɥi sɑ̃]
900 nine hundred	**neuf cents**	[nœf sɑ̃]
1000 one thousand	**mille**	[mil]
10000 ten thousand	**dix mille**	[di mil]
one hundred thousand	**cent mille**	[sɑ̃ mil]
million	**million** (m)	[miljɔ̃]
billion	**milliard** (m)	[miljar]

3. Humans. Family

man (adult male)	**homme** (m)	[ɔm]
young man	**jeune homme** (m)	[ʒœn ɔm]
woman	**femme** (f)	[fam]
girl (young woman)	**jeune fille** (f)	[ʒœn fij]
old man	**vieillard** (m)	[vjɛjar]
old woman	**vieille femme** (f)	[vjɛj fam]
mother	**mère** (f)	[mɛr]
father	**père** (m)	[pɛr]
son	**fils** (m)	[fis]
daughter	**fille** (f)	[fij]
brother	**frère** (m)	[frɛr]
sister	**sœur** (f)	[sœr]
parents	**parents** (pl)	[parɑ̃]
child	**enfant** (m, f)	[ɑ̃fɑ̃]
children	**enfants** (pl)	[ɑ̃fɑ̃]
stepmother	**belle-mère, marâtre** (f)	[bɛlmɛr], [maratr]
stepfather	**beau-père** (m)	[bopɛr]
grandmother	**grand-mère** (f)	[grɑ̃mɛr]
grandfather	**grand-père** (m)	[grɑ̃pɛr]
grandson	**petit-fils** (m)	[pti fis]
granddaughter	**petite-fille** (f)	[ptit fij]
grandchildren	**petits-enfants** (pl)	[pətizɑ̃fɑ̃]
uncle	**oncle** (m)	[ɔ̃kl]
aunt	**tante** (f)	[tɑ̃t]
nephew	**neveu** (m)	[nəvø]
niece	**nièce** (f)	[njɛs]
wife	**femme** (f)	[fam]

husband	**mari** (m)	[mari]
married (masc.)	**marié** (adj)	[marje]
married (fem.)	**mariée** (adj)	[marje]
widow	**veuve** (f)	[vœv]
widower	**veuf** (m)	[vœf]

name (first name)	**prénom** (m)	[prenɔ̃]
surname (last name)	**nom** (m) **de famille**	[nɔ̃ də famij]

relative	**parent** (m)	[parɑ̃]
friend (masc.)	**ami** (m)	[ami]
friendship	**amitié** (f)	[amitje]

partner	**partenaire** (m)	[partənɛr]
superior (n)	**supérieur** (m)	[syperjœr]
colleague	**collègue** (m, f)	[kɔlɛg]
neighbors	**voisins** (m pl)	[vwazɛ̃]

4. Human body

body	**corps** (m)	[kɔr]
heart	**cœur** (m)	[kœr]
blood	**sang** (m)	[sɑ̃]
brain	**cerveau** (m)	[sɛrvo]

bone	**os** (m)	[ɔs]
spine (backbone)	**colonne** (f) **vertébrale**	[kɔlɔn vɛrtebral]
rib	**côte** (f)	[kot]
lungs	**poumons** (m pl)	[pumɔ̃]
skin	**peau** (f)	[po]

head	**tête** (f)	[tɛt]
face	**visage** (m)	[vizaʒ]
nose	**nez** (m)	[ne]
forehead	**front** (m)	[frɔ̃]
cheek	**joue** (f)	[ʒu]

mouth	**bouche** (f)	[buʃ]
tongue	**langue** (f)	[lɑ̃g]
tooth	**dent** (f)	[dɑ̃]
lips	**lèvres** (f pl)	[lɛvr]
chin	**menton** (m)	[mɑ̃tɔ̃]

ear	**oreille** (f)	[ɔrɛj]
neck	**cou** (m)	[ku]
eye	**œil** (m)	[œj]
pupil	**pupille** (f)	[pypij]
eyebrow	**sourcil** (m)	[sursi]
eyelash	**cil** (m)	[sil]
hair	**cheveux** (m pl)	[ʃəvø]

hairstyle	coiffure (f)	[kwafyr]
mustache	moustache (f)	[mustaʃ]
beard	barbe (f)	[barb]
to have (a beard, etc.)	porter (vt)	[pɔrte]
bald (adj)	chauve (adj)	[ʃov]

hand	main (f)	[mɛ̃]
arm	bras (m)	[bra]
finger	doigt (m)	[dwa]
nail	ongle (m)	[ɔ̃gl]
palm	paume (f)	[pom]

shoulder	épaule (f)	[epol]
leg	jambe (f)	[ʒɑ̃b]
knee	genou (m)	[ʒənu]
heel	talon (m)	[talɔ̃]
back	dos (m)	[do]

5. Clothing. Personal accessories

clothes	vêtement (m)	[vɛtmɑ̃]
coat (overcoat)	manteau (m)	[mɑ̃to]
fur coat	manteau (m) de fourrure	[mɑ̃to də furyr]
jacket (e.g., leather ~)	veste (f)	[vɛst]
raincoat (trenchcoat, etc.)	imperméable (m)	[ɛ̃pɛrmeabl]

shirt (button shirt)	chemise (f)	[ʃəmiz]
pants	pantalon (m)	[pɑ̃talɔ̃]
suit jacket	veston (m)	[vɛstɔ̃]
suit	complet (m)	[kɔ̃plɛ]

dress (frock)	robe (f)	[rɔb]
skirt	jupe (f)	[ʒyp]
T-shirt	tee-shirt (m)	[tiʃœrt]
bathrobe	peignoir (m) de bain	[pɛɲwar də bɛ̃]
pajamas	pyjama (m)	[piʒama]
workwear	tenue (f) de travail	[təny də travaj]

underwear	sous-vêtements (m pl)	[suvɛtmɑ̃]
socks	chaussettes (f pl)	[ʃosɛt]
bra	soutien-gorge (m)	[sutjɛ̃gɔrʒ]
pantyhose	collants (m pl)	[kɔlɑ̃]
stockings (thigh highs)	bas (m pl)	[ba]
bathing suit	maillot (m) de bain	[majo də bɛ̃]

hat	chapeau (m)	[ʃapo]
footwear	chaussures (f pl)	[ʃosyr]
boots (cowboy ~)	bottes (f pl)	[bɔt]
heel	talon (m)	[talɔ̃]
shoestring	lacet (m)	[lase]

shoe polish	cirage (m)	[siraʒ]
gloves	gants (m pl)	[gɑ̃]
mittens	moufles (f pl)	[mufl]
scarf (muffler)	écharpe (f)	[eʃarp]
glasses (eyeglasses)	lunettes (f pl)	[lynɛt]
umbrella	parapluie (m)	[paraplɥi]

tie (necktie)	cravate (f)	[kravat]
handkerchief	mouchoir (m)	[muʃwar]
comb	peigne (m)	[pɛɲ]
hairbrush	brosse (f) à cheveux	[brɔs ɑ ʃəvø]

buckle	boucle (f)	[bukl]
belt	ceinture (f)	[sɛ̃tyr]
purse	sac (m) à main	[sak ɑ mɛ̃]

6. House. Apartment

apartment	appartement (m)	[apartəmɑ̃]
room	chambre (f)	[ʃɑ̃br]
bedroom	chambre (f) à coucher	[ʃɑ̃br ɑ kuʃe]
dining room	salle (f) à manger	[sal ɑ mɑ̃ʒe]

living room	salon (m)	[salɔ̃]
study (home office)	bureau (m)	[byro]
entry room	antichambre (f)	[ɑ̃tiʃɑ̃br]
bathroom (room with a bath or shower)	salle (f) de bains	[sal də bɛ̃]
half bath	toilettes (f pl)	[twalɛt]

vacuum cleaner	aspirateur (m)	[aspiratœr]
mop	balai (m) à franges	[balɛ a frɑ̃ʒ]
dust cloth	torchon (m)	[tɔrʃɔ̃]
short broom	balayette (f)	[balɛjɛt]
dustpan	pelle (f) à ordures	[pɛl ɑ ɔrdyr]

furniture	meubles (m pl)	[mœbl]
table	table (f)	[tabl]
chair	chaise (f)	[ʃɛz]
armchair	fauteuil (m)	[fotœj]

mirror	miroir (m)	[mirwar]
carpet	tapis (m)	[tapi]
fireplace	cheminée (f)	[ʃəmine]
drapes	rideaux (m pl)	[rido]
table lamp	lampe (f) de table	[lɑ̃p də tabl]
chandelier	lustre (m)	[lystr]

| kitchen | cuisine (f) | [kɥizin] |
| gas stove (range) | cuisinière (f) à gaz | [kɥizinjɛr ɑ gaz] |

| electric stove | cuisinière (f) électrique | [kɥizinjɛr elɛktrik] |
| microwave oven | four (m) micro-ondes | [fur mikrɔ̃d] |

refrigerator	réfrigérateur (m)	[refriʒeratœr]
freezer	congélateur (m)	[kɔ̃ʒelatœr]
dishwasher	lave-vaisselle (m)	[lavvesɛl]
faucet	robinet (m)	[rɔbinɛ]

meat grinder	hachoir (m)	[aʃwar]
juicer	centrifugeuse (f)	[sɑ̃trifyʒøz]
toaster	grille-pain (m)	[grijpɛ̃]
mixer	batteur (m)	[batœr]

coffee machine	machine (f) à café	[maʃin ɑ kafe]
kettle	bouilloire (f)	[bujwar]
teapot	théière (f)	[tejɛr]

TV set	télé (f)	[tele]
VCR (video recorder)	magnétoscope (m)	[maɲetɔskɔp]
iron (e.g., steam ~)	fer (m) à repasser	[fɛr ɑ rəpase]
telephone	téléphone (m)	[telefɔn]